SOME UNIMAGINABLE ANIMAL

April 2019

Jane,
It's lovely to meet you.
I hope you'll find some words that
SOME *do good things*
UNIMAGINABLE *here —*
ANIMAL

poems by
David Ebenbach

ORISON
BOOKS

Orison Books
PO Box 8385
Asheville, NC 28814
www.orisonbooks.com

ISBN 978-1-949039-23-8

Distributed to the trade by Itasca Books.
1 (800) 901-3480 / orders@itascabooks.com
www.itascabooks.com

Manufactured in the U.S.A.

Cover art: "Monkey" by Daniel McClendon. Used by permission of the
artist. www.danielmcclendon.com

ORISON
BOOKS

Table of Contents

Acknowledgments

Thank you!

I'm talking to you, reader—I am deeply grateful to you for picking up this book to read. You reading the book is, in fact, a fulfillment of a long process from the first drafts of these poems to the finished collection in front of you.

Throughout the process, the work in this book has been buoyed by encouragement and help from many people, and I'm grateful to all of them.

I drafted a number of these poems at the Virginia Center for the Creative Arts. Thank you, VCCA, for your support of so many writers, artists, and composers!

Once the poems were drafted, they needed feedback; thanks so much to the poet Jaimee Kuperman (author of *You Look Nice Strange Man*—such a good book) for her crucial thoughts on nearly every poem in *Some Unimaginable Animal*.

Then the poems, in final draft form, went out into the world on their own, and I am so grateful that many of them found happy homes. Thanks to the journals (and their editors) who published a number of these poems (or versions of these poems) between 2010 and 2018: *Beloit Poetry Journal*, *Beltway Poetry Quarterly*, *DMQ Review*, *DNA*, *Fox Chase Review*, *Gargoyle*, *Iodine Poetry Journal*, *Passages North*, *Poet Lore*, *Poetica*, *Poetry Quarterly*, *Solstice*, *The Southwest Review*, *Stirring*, *Sweet*, and *Thrush Poetry Journal*. And I'm grateful to the artist Kikki Ghezzi for including my poem "Driftwood" in her book *Roots*.

Now these poems are together in a book. Thank you, thank you, Luke Hankins, not only for your careful and thoughtful and expert editorial work throughout the publishing process, but also for your broader work nurturing deep and complex spiritual explorations in poetry and prose. You and Orison Books make the world better.

Of course, my family was here long before the book. Thanks so much to my parents and sister for their consistent support over many years now. (And for teaching me how to eat.) Above all, my biggest thanks go to my wife and my son, without whom—but who would even want to contemplate that? I love you both so much. Thank you.

This book is dedicated to my father,
who taught me that sometimes
the best way to feed the soul
is with actual food.

Basket and Kneading Trough

At lunch we ask what's going to be
for dinner. We snack between meals
to whet our appetite. Hunger is in the mind,
sure, we've all missed out on something,
but food's also just delicious—the cheeses,
the olives, crackers, the big bowls of pasta,
and a soda would be nice. As a treat.
Bring some up from the basement
in case we run out later. Is there pie?
There should be food at the front door—
we deserve it—the house all support staff
for the cabinets, the fridge. Or maybe
we go out, brunch, late dessert, something,
tasting the sweetness of leaving food
for other food. While we're out we see
there's this place or that—you can eat
any country you want, sometimes buffet.
Not to mention the grocery stores, the bodegas!
By the time we get home—the restaurant
had three menus in sequence—we've
been through something. We're tired.
We stand at the front door with a key
in the lock, pausing. We can smell the food
on the other side. Waiting.

Change

We were throwing our little sins
at the ceiling, hoping
they would stick. But they didn't
even get there; as soon as
they were airborne our sins started
buzzing around
in these drunken, staggering loops.
One might hum in
behind your ear and then be gone
when you whirled
around. Or you might smack one
dead on your forearm
and leave behind a little spot of
your own blood.
It was frustrating; we could barely
concentrate on
repentance. What we really needed
was a bunch of
bats ready in the rafters, hungry
and blind enough to eat
anything they could get their jaws on.
We certainly
lobbed enough sins to draw them out.
We flung them with
everything we had. But there were
no bats. Or,
if there were, they were still
asleep.

Things Are Very Far Apart

I mean the moon,
                    the sun—
I mean everything. The universe

is empty as a bowl

but without
the bowl. A little dust
                    doesn't

crowd a room.

          Space was
          named for itself.

And yet it's full as a bowl.

Here we are, strung
          to that boiling
pivot,

ninety-three million miles

away
          but still bound,

and there's enough
light here that

everything lives, and sees,

and if you looked at that light, you

          wouldn't
see anything
else.   Here we are, all

nothing even to the moon

and still
the oceans try to rise to it.

The First Debate

The universe banged open, pretty soon the size
of an auditorium, and the debaters took their places—

energy arcing from one end of the stage to the other,
matter moving only as it was moved, pulled
by the whole thing's expansion, gravely toward the infinite.

Like all debates, they talked past each other; energy
kept turning the lights off and on while matter
held up one solid molecule after another. And energy
made matter go, and matter gave energy something to do.

It didn't make any difference. Everything was everywhere,
without knowing it. By now the stage was bigger than an idea.
There were a lot more voices.

If Eden Had Been a City

If Eden had been a city God could have relaxed,
planted the apple tree in front of row houses
and Adam and Eve would have walked right by,
down to where the corner store would have had
bottled juice and mini-pies and cider donuts.
They would sit out on their front steps with some
nice beats coming out of the window, faces sticky
with flavors, dazed and looking at all the different
skinny trees up and down the block, still springtime,
thinking, *Damn, this is good*. They would be full,
too full for trouble. Nearby, a stray cat would stalk
the patchy grass along the curb, making quick work
of anything that slithered.

City of Worry

Out running, my shoes collect the fresh trash
of gingko fruit, back again for the third time—
the trees don't know what season it is.
We've gotten so bad at winter. We leave our
sweaters in a pile by the door. There are days
when I consider sandals, though not without
guilt. Running, breath gratefully cloudy
this morning, a sign that December might be
out of its depression and ready to sit up in bed.
We are the heavy blankets. The exhaust. We
are the winter's growing *why bother*. It's uphill
past the out-of-use estate and its trees, uphill
on these zagging bricks. Some of the trees
have leaves. We're ruining them for the next
windstorm. Which is coming, they say tomorrow.
I'm running for home. Even if the air is cold
in the labor of my lungs, we can't get used
to that. It's still morning, lots of sun coming.
After that, something else.

Sukkot

We dwell, as ever, in tents.
It's the Book Festival
again, the Mall restless
with covered pavilions
and overhung with clouds
that preach illiteracy.
Wind shapes all these walls,
then shapes them
again. The first tent
is where they sell the books
that are just now being opened,
sell them off folding tables
planted in the grass. Here
people gather
what they might love.
Elsewhere people
read themselves aloud
under the shifting cover
to rows of unfolded chairs.
Our senses tell us,
This is happening.
The old wisdom tells us,
You'll live like this for seven days,
in homes
that cannot stand. But these
days are more than lifetimes;
the world, which
won't stand either,
was built in seven of them.
Willful, we find the right place,
we take our seats
and listen to what we mean to hear.
The tables are stacked
with tote bags, with clutches
of paper.

Habitats

We knew about this when we signed the lease, though we couldn't know
what it meant, just *better units by winter*, no sense of what it is to live
in work: crowd scenes in the hallways, on all sides of the building
a haze of smoke breaks, and always the sound of heavy tools,
construction the same as demolition to our ears. They have to
turn the water off for a day, the power. And at some point
the heat is off until whenever they can give it back to us,
new.
      When they start in our apartment we see how near
is that sense of eviction—a few holes in the ceiling
and walls, furniture under plastic, a grit of plaster dust
in the teeth: we don't live here. The floor goes white
under our feet, our bedsheets turn to chalk.
                             But that's
temporary, and we do want better heat. What lasts
is that tenuous grip. The workers clear out, back
into the hallways, and we replant our stake
at the edge of the worksite. Construction chases
bugs and mice into our kitchen and bathroom.
They live here, too, but with less pretense.
Home? One safe hole is as good as another.
They are so fragile. And it's just a hole,
just a place to stop moving until you
have to start moving again.

The First Insect

The first insect must have been
lonely; this was way before swarming.
They say that the first insect had
a very general mouth, good for eating
anything. Those were the times.
There may have been wings, though
you can't tell from the fossils; maybe
the first insect just had flying dreams
like the rest of us. The first insect
probably started small. Maybe it sat there
working its very general jaw, testing it,
trying one food after the next.

From Scratch

Some people, you go to their house for dinner
and there's no dinner, there's cooking. These are
the kind of people who have every implement,
have an opinion on garlic presses, for sure
know the difference between a spatula
and a turner, have stories about where they got
this spice or the one in the little sachet. They
pour you a glass of something, probably good,
and say, Hang out with us in the kitchen
while we finish things up. Steam from pots
rolls up into the steel oven hood, plus the smell
of the sauté pan working. There's nowhere to sit
so you lean against a counter they just had done,
but it's got a sharp or a hard edge. Sometimes
they've got a stool and you swing your legs
and think about the snacks you didn't have
before you left. Though there might be nibbles
along the way—try this, does it need anything?—
and drinking's efficient on an empty stomach.
You haven't home-made anything, ever.
When you cook, it's like stapling one ingredient
to another, dry and askew. Eventually it's nine-
thirty, and the bread has cooled and the soup is
perfectly milled and the sauces have all thickened,
and it's time. That's when a sadness comes over
the kitchen, which you almost don't catch, you're
so hungry: the cooks are done. They're done
and the cooking was the pleasure part, so now
their pleasure is just some food. Now it's just
the tedious rotating of jaws, the steady dis-
assembly of what matters. If they could, if you
would let them, they'd scrape the full plates
and start something else. There are ramekins;
there are cooking torches waiting in the drawer.
They only want to use them.

Pride Before the Meal

Sometimes what I want is a sticky bun that's world famous
according to the restaurant's owner in small-town Pennsylvania,
or yogurt that has been declared the country's best, but not by
a panel of experts. Sometimes I want food braggadocio.
And not the verifiable—I can see for myself when a burrito is
bigger than my head—but the totally subjective; this guy's
carrot cake will ruin you for all others, especially the one
down the block. Everyone knows that pizzeria; this soup
will haunt your dreams.

Other times I want a diner that shrugs and calls itself
A Place for Ribs. There are others, the owner knows. Or like
a restaurant that brags, *If there were gold medals for comfort,
we bet our food would be a semifinalist*. There is virtue
in the understatement. *We hope you'll enjoy!* There is a sweetness
to a rice pudding that, hey, is one of the rice puddings
of the universe, there for people who like that sort of thing.
A bar promises warm beer and cold food, and they deliver.

It all works: sometimes the menu promises riches and so you
sit down with the Gods; sometimes the waitress shrugs
and you're on your own. *Gods don't eat*, she says. *People do.*

The Back of God's Head

And God said: "Here is a place with Me....I will cover you with My hand until I have passed by. And I will take away My hand, and you will see My back; but My face will not be seen."

Exodus 33:21-23

Late Friday afternoon and the cicadas roll sound
over the wash of cars from Route 29, plus
someone's playing *Let's stay together*
in another part of the valley, loud enough
for the mountains to share. It's still daytime,
indirectly. Everything is first shadow.
Sometimes it must be a truck on the highway,
the *unnn* of industry, and the insects overhead
are working as hard as ever. They don't put down
their tools. They don't know Al Green, even if
they're bent the same way toward persuasion.
Evening takes a step. Out across the lawn
grass reaches up unhurried, moved by the wind
that holds the note.

Like a Fuel

I keep thinking about how boring sunsets must have been
before pollution. In the heart of the Renaissance, not much
there worth painting—slice of dull orange, and then darkness.

Though of course they had all the stars, like what we have
along country roads when the car breaks down, but more,
so you could see those old Greek dogs and bears.

But probably everyone was asleep at night. It was hard work
to live five hundred years ago. You took down crops with
scythes. Some days you were just dragging over cobblestones.

In our time we've traded the body in for the internal
combustion engine. And though we drag some days along
asphalt, still we send up our incense, and that's why our sky
burns, like a fuel.

Dwelling

The train passes a field of house-outlines,
just the frames, cream wood at right angles
and a few with walls of insulation but nowhere
a roof; everything is still outdoors.

In the fall we live in frames ourselves, *Ye shall*
dwell in booths seven days, a week of admitting
to the temporary. We eat under branches
unless there's enough rain to spoil the soup.

But these will become houses; roads
will turn in here. While we hammer together
ritual that comes in pieces and that can
always be disassembled again.

A home makes us believe it's not raining.
Tradition taps at the window-glass.

Late Afternoon

and rain comes in like dusk—in no hurry, clouds
dimming the lights by slow degrees, so that my thoughts
start to set, turn to put the day away.

And it starts to fall, not night but the sound of
rushing water against the parking lot, the apartment
greying and ready, lunch dishes quiet in the sink.

But when the rain slows, the day steps back in
for a moment. I stop, caught—in my hands the day's hours,
wrapped in my willingness to be done with them.

Page-Turner

I'm going to write a *whodunit*, but in this one
you'll know who the murderer is, right away;
what you'll have to figure out is who they killed.
And so the detective will gather the suspects
in the living room, will interview them one
by one. The elderly baroness who never
became a pilot, the butler with gout and the driver
who loves him in futility. Maid, minister,
and the child born in sin; the cousin just back
from darkest Sweden. Each one
smoking or playing cards or eating too much.
Each one just a shade off vivid. The detective
looks for clues, some whiff of the expired.
The classic ruse: just as he seems
on the verge of revealing the truth, his assistant
cuts the lights. And while everyone else
launches into a clatter of existential debate—
what *is* darkness, and whence our innocent
belief in the day?—the hapless murdered sighs
a sigh. The detective follows the sound and,
as the lights come back on, stands there before
the body, which finally slumps, only now
admitting to its own decomposure.

The Philosopher Points

and asks them, *What am I pointing at?* The obvious answer
is *that table*, but it's the sixth week of class and he knows
they've learned to doubt their instincts. So he says it for them:
How do you know—this is how he starts almost everything—
*I'm pointing at that table? How do you know I'm not pointing
at brown?* and he waits for that to sink in. Their faces are like
dry erase boards. *Or flatness, or just down, or even the air
right in front of my finger?* He only wants them to know
that they don't know anything. His pointing hand is dusty
with chalk. And of course his own instinct tells him that's
a table there, and he remembers when the department finally
got approval for new tables. This one is conference-style,
has that fake wood veneer. He could be pointing at sameness,
or the decline of American craftsmanship. The students are silent,
waiting stoic for him to pluck their last pieces of knowledge
out of the air. Sometimes he sees that he's like a depressing
magician at a kid's birthday party. Maybe he's pointing at
dust—the air is full of dust, chalk and otherwise. He says,
How do you know I'm pointing at anything at all? and he
knows he's taking it too far. Someone will surely protest: *But
you said. You asked us.* But the magic is strong, and they
just wait for him to finish. He dismisses them. After they're
gone, he stays in the room. He continues to point, aiming his
chalk-dusty finger now at floor and ceiling, at space; at beige,
fluorescence, and straight; smoothness, break, and flaw; one
by one making them vanish, and fail to disappear.

In the Halls After Class

Students process like monks, like penitents,
staring down at their phones—
those black mirrors,
those rosaries—
their smoothness thumbed smooth.
An hour, more, spent
at the chore of stillness, of desks,
spent between urgent thoughts.
They are emerging from whatever contemplation
they built in those rooms.
No sound now, but the air
fills with their answers,
their questions.

Civilization

I wonder if dolphins get enough from life, or if
they're discontented, too, but with useless flippers.
They want their fish cooked, maybe, or somewhere
cozy to sleep—they'd like to see what land's like—
but all they can do is circle and sometimes leap
back into the same water.

The First Mammal

The first mammal was only a little
hairy. Its blood wasn't warm yet,
or cold still, but more like room
temperature. The first mammal lived
on a rock, gasping at all
the changes. It was surrounded
by an ocean, or teeth; scientists
now believe that the first mammal
only had time to make two babies
before something ate it, or a wave
swept it away. The babies
looked each other over
through their growing bangs.
The first mammal slipped away
in the closing, receding mouth
of whatever. The sky was very cloudy.
Two creatures staying warm.

Whale, Extinct

According to these bones, this was
all water. Where we're standing in our
waterproof boots, in the Perkins Geology Museum,
was ocean, everything under the press of the Champlain.
This long, alien skull—at first mistaken for horse
by the railroad worker whose shovel struck bone—this skull
looks like a hundred pounds, but it once floated through the brack
hungry, and died that way.
                                        And what after that?
The sea recedes again, inevitably, the drying sand strewn
with new bone—and all of us, or what remains, left to
some unimaginable animal and its tools of excavation.
And then sea again, and then land, until at some
point there are no more animals left to dig.
Do you understand that, lost whale? That
we will then no longer be here, none of us,
none, that finally it's just the land and the ocean,
continuing their longer argument, our bones only loose
teeth in this debate? What changes? The land says
land, the sea comes all the way back to say *sea*.

Driftwood

What's this? the boy asks
in his infinitesimal voice. It's fall,
they're at the foot of the dunes,
the reeds nodding over them.
Mom is still in bed.
This is driftwood, the father says,
touching and then picking up
the chunk of tree limb—
all elbows and knots,
no better word for it than *gnarl*.
But what is *it?* the boy asks.
And the father explains
this was once a branch,
somehow it got into the sea,
he doesn't know how—oh,
the things fathers should
know—but the water skinned
the wood, opened seams in it,
left it here for the sun
to whiten through its daily examinations.
The father holds the awkward
fragment. He doesn't get into
how *we* started out like this,
some remote ancestor no longer fish,
some gnarled
origin, some knobby limb
crawling up from one version of life
into another. Doesn't say
that the boy, too, was like this
in the beginning,
pale and crouched
at the foot of the unknown
world. The father can't speak
past the object
in his throat. Anyway
the boy is done with the driftwood.

He's moved off to a clamshell—
half a body, an open
bowl.

Sometimes It's Like This

After breakfast, I take a train,
and by the time I'm back it's night,
and you're asleep in our bed.

When I wake up the next morning,
you're on a train, and you
won't be back until dinner.

Sometimes it's like this—
one of us moving, the other still.

But tonight I'll make us something
to eat. I'll sauté spinach, use garlic,
make a nest for the black beans.

When you open the door,
you'll be ready to eat. And steam
will be rising off the plates.

While They Choose a New Pope, I Eat a Bagel

These are old occupations. In Vatican City there is no
wi-fi, not until after they've sent their white smoke
rising. Black smoke means they're still at it. Here
it would mean the bagel's burning. There's no white kind.
They used to carry them around on sticks, which is why
the hole in the middle, and we keep it even though
sometimes the butter ends up pooling right in the center
of the plate. We keep things the way they are.
The Cardinals—do they sit around a table, a dark table
older than America? They may have bagels of their own,
though it's hard to imagine them licking cream cheese
off their thumbs. But things do change. They used to
lock the bishops in the chapel until they got it done, and now
there are hotels and buses. They wake up to a coffee maker,
maybe a continental breakfast. And I've got a toaster,
and a food processor to make the hummus, everything
I need. There may be windows high up in the wall,
shuttered. Nobody's allowed to see things in process.
The Cardinals crowd around, one of them almost a Pope. Me,
I'm already eating the bagel.

The Flower

The poet from Iran
was born before her parents,
is what the interpreter says.
It means she knows everything.
When we give her the tour,
she says, Let's go inside,
where she keeps wearing her
white coat. In the campus chapel
under the new ceiling, beside the new
stained glass, she asks me
if I go to church every week
and I have to say I'm Jewish.
She takes the quietest step
backward. And when we get to the room
where she's going to read she sits
in the row in front of me and turns to say,
Sorry to give you my back.
What you say in Iran, I know, is
A flower has no back.

Outside the White House, the Muezzin Calls Us to Prayer

To the things not of this world, that is. In any case
there is no laundry, white or otherwise, clean or not,
hanging over this street, everything wide open,
from the empty lawn in front of the House that is white
to the unadorned fence that surrounds it, to the clean, quieted street:
no sounds of the city, no traffic except tourists on foot,
only the muteness of that House that's off from us. Meanwhile
there's a man in white, his voice
hanging its quavering balance in the air,
and he turns his voice and his long banner—
There Is No God But God—in four directions, as though
folding the Earth's corners together. If they will come.
A few tourists break from their bright clumps to step close,
to photograph him. Rather, they take his picture
away. The only car is a parked police cruiser,
pointed East. No-one else approaches. There is
no sound of pulleys, no swinging wide of the black gates,
no word from the House or its empty lawn.
The man touches his forehead
to the rough macadam of the street.

City of Wilderness

There are no cities. Just these
breaks in the trees, and all the animals—
the mice on their migratory routes
across the kitchen floor, the chimney
swifts making circles overhead—
There's a buck in the parking lot,
many-pointed, sharp head up among
all the cars and their paint jobs.
Behind him, the ground slopes back
into the woods, while against the brick
of the apartment building, a doe. She's
nibbling at the landscaping. She's
the reason he's here. And has been,
since long before this landscape
got made out of plants.

Fauna

Fauna: the animals characteristic of a region, period, or special environment.

Merriam-Webster

Once that summer my sister woke me, panicking
about the rat on the porch, which turned out to be
a ferret, a lost pet. We had ferrets at the zoo,

smart animals with sharp eyes. Out of bounds,
it was like my job at the children's zoo following me
home, the smell of pony I couldn't wash off

and that hung with me on the bus rides through
torn-up Mantua. We lived just past that,
in West Philadelphia, where we also didn't fit.

At the zoo we had opossums, too, which were
vicious and dumb, so that when I cleaned their cages
I had to distract them with a steel brush and

yank them out by their too-strong tails, shaking them
so they didn't pull up for a chunk of my arm.
I had read about animals, and when they trained us

I knew the genealogy of the wolf. I could tell you
what pilot whales knew. One morning I saw
an opossum on our porch, on my way out to work.

Now, that was the face of a rat. Animals were mixed up
all over—the dead-end mule at the pony track;
the squirrels too used to popcorn, the raccoons I saw

at dusk, part cat, part bear, lumbering along the curb.

On the Day We Dissected a Cat

I couldn't find anything. The teaching assistant
said something like, *After you remove*
the vernacular, you will see the green rolling hills
of the minor antipodes, and so on, and I stared
into what seemed like the mouth of the cat,
like everything was the mouth,
like wherever you opened a cat it would be
another mouth, but filled with oatmeal and mucus.
The teaching assistant came over
and pointed a stick—it was like a kabob skewer—
and said, *See? There.* He pointed at one lump.
There's the danube. And I said, *Can you just*
show me the lungs, the heart, some place
to work from? And he sighed. The kabob skewer
hopped from flesh to flesh. *Lung lung heart*
kidney kidney stomach. He was bored
of those organs, which even themselves
I only glimpsed momentarily, breaching like
distant whales, before I lost them again.
The teaching assistant went back to the head table
and told us, *Now we're looking for*
the bicameral taverna. Everyone hunched down
over their trays. I stared into the cat's open mouths.

Hunger

But not the hunger of the afternoon
too long at the desk, hands adrum
before the computer—

and not the hunger of the fast,
the plan, your fridge full
of what you won't eat—

not even the four-in-the-morning
hunger, shocked hollow in the gut,
but sleep cures it—

no, not the temporary hunger,
the blood-sugar plummet,
the stage play—

instead the long hunger,
the hunger of the march
and the door that won't lock—

the hunger at the edge
of a slow paycheck. Real hunger,
with a jaw of its own—

The First Primate

Life was tough for the first primate.
The first primate clung to bark
knowing that all it took
was one loose grip, and it was back
to the forest floor. Where there's
no point in being a primate,
so the first primate hooked claws
deep and used its puffy tail
for balance, and waited for things
to become clearer. Overhead, leaves
shook like so many hands.
But the old kind of hands.

In the Museum of Natural History

It's a weekday morning because I'm out of work,
the halls empty, just me, tired, and this Neanderthal

in fossil, this frame of a person who's outlasted
everyone he ever knew: his clan's man of wisdom

who read other bones, the hunter who
forced so many mammoths off the cliffs.

Even their best storyteller, who remembered it all.
But this man is here because he died

in the sediment of the river they never crossed.
No great accomplishment, disappearing,

the clan still in the cave, this one wading too far,
and for no reason we can know. Maybe he was

bored. Maybe lost. Do any of us know why we go
where we go? I stand there a long time, shifting

my feet on the marble floors. *You are the only
famous Neanderthal*, I think. *It doesn't matter why*.

If We Came From Fish, Why Are There Still Fish?

The interpreter is lost in traffic, but there's always
a camera, ready to quote people unsparingly. They fill
separate hallways, God and no-God, fill big sketchpads
with only the rhetorical: *So how do you explain a sunset?*
The beauty? and *Do you really believe in a talking*
snake? They write *Carbon dating* and *Noetics* in large
letters. Can they get a witness? Someone pounds
a podium, and half the crowd says *Yes, oh yes.*
What it comes down to is the books, again in their
two stacks: the ones you have to burn, and the ones
that have started to burn without you. Smoke
in both lungs.

I Don't Have to Be Right for You to Be Wrong

I'm going to write a book on religious intolerance—
a how-to. It's going to have thought exercises,
like *Isn't your neighbor's god pretty much
hilarious?* and role-playing scenarios, like
practice smiting or at least rolling your eyes when
anyone else starts talking. Plus maybe some lists
of what everybody else is dumb as shit about.
I mean, that's your afterlife? Thousands of years,
and that's your story? I'm going to recommend
focused meditation where people accept duality.
Maybe a chapter on seeing things from the other guy's
point of view and laughing about it. Of course,
a lot of that is filler; but nobody's going to buy a book
that just says, *Keep up the good work.*

After the Battle

They moved farther into the land and came across what first appeared to be a mountain but was in fact an extraordinary, mountainous knot. The knot was so vast that they supposed it would take them two days to march around it. So they camped there at its foot to decide what they ought to do next, and endured a night that was utterly dark yet filled with the uncertain intimations of voices. In the morning they began their attempts to untie the knot; one of them had suggested that the voices were promising riches or other destinies in the knot's deep interior. It quickly became clear that the rope, as thick as ten men together, was made up of many thinner strands, that each of those strands was knotted to others, that indeed there were countless thousands of knots at the heart of this one mountainous knot. They started to work in earnest, all of them picking and grasping and in fact tearing at it. They continued into the night with its voices, and into the days beyond. This is how their enemies found them, and how the battle was engaged once more. With one hand they pulled at the knot and with the other they swung the sword. Their enemies, too, found themselves caught between a desire for vengeance and a desire to disentangle. Because war never fails utterly, blood was shed. It soaked into the ropes and, as it dried, tightened them, first around hands, then around arms and bodies. By this time, all were quite unable to move. Nonetheless, the fighting found a way to continue, and the knot continued to tighten.

Monsters

They surface like a judgment, these ugliest fish
anyone has ever seen. Almost B-movie, the way they
roll up from the murk, scales the waxy yellow
of the embalmed, to suck wide-mouthed at the bread
chunks we've scattered across the water, now froth
and churn. And we, B-movie characters ourselves,
came here because we are not innocent. It's fall,
the pond still unfrozen, our hands ready to cast off
old uses. The bread meant to float off toward
vanishing. Instead this frenzy, these grotesques,
heavy bodies clashing to feed on what we're
giving them.

Howling

What it's really about is that we all want a secret,
an *Oh, if you only knew me*. Because maybe
we're not just the guy who eats a cold lunch at his desk
and feels it sit cold in his mouth
while he works up the guts to chew, not just the guy
who climbs the stairwell between office floors
because it takes longer and there's time to think about
what else might have happened. Not just the guy
who takes the bus and even the bus gets stuck in traffic.
Maybe we're the guy who turns to the woman
taking up too much seat next to him
and bites down into the shoulder. Oh, sure,
it'd be a life of blood and regret. But at least
the moon might be watching.

Procedural Drama

I'm going to write my own procedural drama.
Mostly it'll be the same as the other ones:
first, the dead body, discovered by teenagers
in an alley, or by the maid in a gilt bedroom,
or at the feet of joggers in a gentrifying park.
Then the police officers, delivering the sad
news, surreptitiously pressing the loved ones,
and then other suspects, until it all clarifies.
But then the trial, where despite the evidence
the careerist defense attorney brings motion
after motion, suppressing the crucial facts.
All the while we know who did it, and maybe
why. We just want it proven publicly, just
want the win, want the murderer shut away.
And, like the other shows, the main characters
will never develop, episode to episode—
each time they'll shake their heads cynically
at the body, pursue relentlessly, curse
the defense attorney, stoically accept the victory.
But then, each time, everyone—the family
of the victim, sure, but also the district attorney
and the cops—they'll all go back to the alley,
the bed, the park, and there they'll fall
to the ground, wailing helplessly: *Still dead!*
they'll cry. *Still dead! Still dead!*

Age

The cheese has gone blue in the drawer
when I get back from visiting hours;
the cherry tomatoes are wrinkled
as skin. One morning I sat up
through an arc of pain as high
as my shoulder. And the old man
is still learning to walk, hopefully as well as
a child. We go wrong.
Hard to watch with these eyes, blurring.
The vinegar of accumulated causes.
Now, shoulder quiet for the moment,
I bag the lost—yogurt, leftovers—
until the fridge is near empty. The next day
the old man is at his walker. We say he's
regaining something. He's across
the room. Small steps
take more effort, the nurse tells us,
holding his belt.

The Meadow Burns

A meadow learns nothing without fire

Clyde Kessler

and at some point the fire doesn't go out.
This is adulthood; gone are the forgotten tragedies,
the ones that take a little skin, replaceable,
and fade. Even the scar is just a story of old heat.
Now we've got the wounds that stay open, panting.
There's a first one, the first compromise between
you and what's actually in front of you. You hold
some hand, some old root, while the smoke
piles up, the low music. All around, the meadow
is learning a long lesson. And that's when
it doesn't come: the cooling breeze, the rain,
the salve or bandage, the rough stitch closed.

Visitation

The men take smoke breaks
outside the funeral home, where
sheets of January wind scatter
their ashes. Inside, the line
moves slowly. Person after person
approaches the family with the same
offerings. Waiting are the sister,
the fiancé, the parents. They stand
for two hours. Beyond them
is the urn, actually a wooden box,
but too small to contain anyone real.
Not even a newborn, which she
never had. We glance terror
in that direction. Soon a priest
will tell us what happened here.
Outside winter presses, but everyone
has come inside. They carry smoke.

Snowstorm

The snow will look the other way
and settle in our gardens,
layer everything we've built.
We brace ourselves, as if for a beating,
while the clouds unroll north
because they have to be somewhere;
and they didn't mean to pack so much luggage.
Under the kitchen counters we line the shelves
with jugs of water. There'll be water outside,
of course, but you can't use it.
It has no use for us, either.
It'll cover what was here before us. It'll pull under
what we've left in place. Tomorrow
the schools will close and we'll be saying
the same things we always have. Like praying. We'll
drag our tiny shovels through the white
and start to sweat.

Our Memory for a Blessing Right Now

Do you know that Samuel Beckett play
where a woman gives birth into a grave?
I'm going to write a poem about death,
death being nothing like they tell you
on TV. There is no cloak or scythe, no
slim elegance. The whole thing is more
like melting. Which is why it happens
to everyone, and which is why it happens
all the time—your eyes, your lungs,
the ankle that goes. You wake up
into unexpected pains, your body a new
obstacle. Some people say Beckett's play
is a poem, but some people say
a sunset's a poem. Meanwhile, I'm sitting
in a chair that's slowly compressing
my spine—everything slow before stop,
a steady dimmer switch.

Ghost Stories

I'm going to write a Jewish one, a ghost story
without equilibrium. Because let's face it:
most of those tales believe in a God who keeps
a tally. The equations always balance—
possession only in stolen homes, chains
on the stairs of people who can't stop grasping.
If you lust, you die in your panties. In those stories,
sin is a paranormal boomerang, and no room for
the accident, the coincidence, or for the people
who know to expect the worst regardless.
So in my story there will be the haunting
of the innocent. Floorboards will creak their way
to people just eating breakfast. Doing laundry.
Some of the victims will deserve it, sure,
but by accident. When the chandelier falls they'll
stand underneath like anyone else, in a circle
of wonder like a bull's-eye, or passing ripples
in a pond of no opinions. The lights tremble,
but in your house, too.

Hanukkah

This year we spangle the place, the door
wrapped like something we're giving away,
the whole living room wrapped,
coffee table a jumble of wind-up toys
and candy dishes,
the seam of the wall into ceiling
a braid of lights, illuminating
plastic chunks of holiday
kitsch. The bookshelves, the rug,
everything is plastic now, is sequins,
is glitter. Stars and dreidles, dreidles and stars.
Everything held up with tape. Meanwhile
the gifts are underfoot
in every direction. And sure we make it
dark, lightswitch by lightswitch, unplug
the string of bulbs, let the candles
make their quiet points.
                              But then we
plug the strings back in,
and tap the uncooperative set
until it works.

The Rabbi's Advice

The old cow lows close to the little kitchen woodstove, though for once it's not cold in here, and that cry fills the room to the walls, but it's the sound of goats all around that shudders the bones, and we don't dare move for fear of slipping. It's only a three-room cottage as it is, my Sarah and me who sleep in one room, our too-many daughters in the other, and here in the kitchen our son Jacob. Plus Sarah's parents, who have the bed in our room, and we the floor. Bring the livestock in, the rabbi said. He expects me to wonder about his sanity—I came to him because I needed room to draw air into my lungs, at least, and now he's filled our house with animals. But I know he'll tell me to add the chickens next, and maybe double the mice somehow. I know that when I'm about to collapse altogether he'll tell me to take all the animals out, and, look how spacious my life actually is. This is how we think here—it could always be worse. But I almost don't see the animals, even now. I see my parents-in-law sitting at the table, shaking, still cold and getting colder. We have no money to bury them. Jacob is pressed to the window, his hatred of this house its own loud lowing. My daughters are years from marriage and always moments from terror, about it happening and about it not. My wife Sarah's hands are aging while she sews. If it wasn't a goat nibbling on our socks, it would be time. Or what about my own hands, raw from the udders. The animals walk around us almost gingerly, around my anger, the clumsy table and chairs.

Everything's Going to Be Okay

I'm going to write one of those novels you can't
put down. The kind where you don't know what's
going to happen, and you want to know what's
going to happen, so you sneak the book into
the bathroom to get a few pages in while your wife
thinks you're brushing your teeth or showering,
or you take it to work and hope your workstation
walls are high enough to keep the book secret.
It's going to be a threat to your marriage and your
livelihood, this book, though it'll probably also
cut down on overeating and any drinking problems,
because who has time for any of that when you're
racing to find out whether the main character gets
away, or love, or the bad guy? You'll want to rip
and chew your way to the end of the book, just to
find out. Though, seriously, we both know what's
going to happen: the main character is going to get
away, and love, and the bad guy. That's why you
bought the book, why you let your life fall apart
to read it: Because you know that somewhere
in the universe things are in good order; somewhere
justice moves forward and doesn't flip back.

Passover This Year

It finally snows, five days after
the first day of spring, and we're like,
where have you been, because by now
we've shelved the snow angels.
We were thinking more like cherry blossoms.
The fact is we've adjusted our calendars;
seven leap months in nineteen years,
because this is supposed to be spring.

So anyway we sit down together
at a table where everything's renewal,
renewal, and under the table our boots
slush the floor and leave salt footprints.
Well, we're used to contradiction;
there's salt water on the table, too.
We carry our tears with us, in little bowls.
We lug them across national borders
and the calendar. Meanwhile, the snow
follows us just to say, get over yourselves,
we all have our problems.

Happiness

Sometimes when you pause to speak of it,
it turns from you like a shy child, so that you're
left reaching, talking about those ready fill-ins:
loss and the particular cold wind kicked up by
what passes. Afterward, you know you've
blown it again, walking home silent, happiness
dragging a pace behind. *We practiced this,*
you say. It turns up that face that says it's sorry
without knowing why. You walk that way
a long time. But then you get home, and it's
mid-afternoon, nothing much you have to do,
so you sit down together at the table, pour cereal
into bowls, giant bowls too big for just cereal,
but you pour them full, and cold milk all the way
to the top. It's the way the bowl goes cool in
your hands, the absolute quiet of the apartment.
What is there to say? You eat—just cereal, but
there's plenty.

The Ineffable

Maybe we should just stick to food. Or anyway
the body. There's not a lot more out there—
sometimes I think the world stops at my teeth,
and then I eat it. And the rest of time is grand
illusion. Walk up the steps, ascend—
that's your feet—and take whatever honey
you can hold in one hand.

This Happened To Me

It was one of those days in March
where I just wore a light jacket because
I didn't mind being a little cold
and optimistic, and then it turned out
I didn't even need the jacket. Outside
people were at outdoor tables, metal
outdoor chairs, leaning into them like
into cushions. The forecasters
were predicting a half a foot overnight,
but during this day dogs were
at the distant ends of their leashes, dogs
everywhere. The lights changed
and people rambled into crosswalks.
We opened shop doors, windows.
We were just going to have to
close them up again later, but it was
fine. I'm telling you, this happened
to me. Other things, too, but let's
start with this.

ABOUT THE AUTHOR

David Ebenbach is the author of the novel *Miss Portland*, selected by Peter Orner for The 2016 Orison Poetry Prize, and three short story collections: *The Guy We Didn't Invite to the Orgy and Other Stories* (winner of the Juniper Prize, University of Massachusetts Press), *Between Camelots* (winner of the Drue Heinz Literature Prize, University of Pittsburgh Press), and *Into the Wilderness* (Winner of the Washington Writers Publishing House Fiction Prize, WWPH). He is also the author of a full-length collection of poetry, *We Were the People Who Moved* (Winner of the Patricia Bibby Prize, Tebot Bach) and a guide to the creative process called *The Artist's Torah* (Cascade Books). Ebenbach holds a PhD in Psychology from the University of Wisconsin-Madison and an MFA in Writing from Vermont College. He teaches creative writing at Georgetown University.

ABOUT ORISON BOOKS

Orison Books is a 501(c)3 non-profit literary press focused on the life of the spirit from a broad and inclusive range of perspectives. We seek to publish books of exceptional poetry, fiction, and non-fiction from perspectives spanning the spectrum of spiritual and religious thought, ethnicity, gender identity, and sexual orientation.

As a non-profit literary press, Orison Books depends on the support of donors. To find out more about our mission and our books, or to make a donation, please visit www.orisonbooks.com.

Orison Books thanks Eric Dimick Eastman for his
financial support of this book.

To support upcoming Orison Books titles, please visit
www.orisonbooks.com/support-a-book, or write to
Luke Hankins at editor@orisonbooks.com.